The Deserts of Africa

The Deserts of Africa

Photographs and text by **Michael Martin**

Foreword by **Malidoma and Sobunfu Somé**

Translated from the German by **Anthea Bell**

STEWART, TABORI & CHANG

NEW YORK

Foreword

The land mass of the African continent is as rich in variety as is its population: a boundless expanse of geographical and cultural diversity stretching all the way from the Atlas Mountains south of the Mediterranean down to the Cape of Good Hope, it contains more deserts than any other part of the world, including the Sahara, the Kalahari and the Namib, to mention only the most familiar. Since access is difficult, and most of all because of the sense of emptiness that many people associate with deserts, they represent a great challenge to those who seek to know more about them. Yet that apparent emptiness holds profound social and spiritual wisdom, which could be of great benefit to the world – something of humanity's most valuable and indeed sacred inheritance.

The word "desert" usually conjures up images of barren desolation, of a place from which life is almost entirely absent. One envisages a bleak and god-forsaken wilderness never intended for mankind. This negative image is partly the result of historical conditioning. History has done Africa and its population no favours here, and Western books tend to depict the continent in a gloomy light, except when promoting the opportunities it offers for enjoyable safaris and when dwelling on the attractive natural resources to which Europeans are still drawn. For centuries – from the days of open slavery to colonial times – misleading propaganda aimed to portray the African as weak and lacking in dignity; as a result, Africans have often been regarded as third-class citizens in the world, always overshadowed by the West. The present book, *The Deserts*

Street boy in the Sudan. His face, hands and clothes are blackened from carrying sacks of charcoal.

of Africa, seeks to redress the balance, emphasizing those aspects of the continent – its beauty and capacity for inspiration – to which little attention has yet been paid. For all who wish to explore the deep wisdom of the African continent, the deserts of Africa are an ideal point of departure: in these places, the strength, power and dignity of Africa's people are abundantly clear.

The pictures in this book display this. They should be viewed not with the eye of a geologist, but with a sense of awe and respect for their sublime mysteries, colourful immediacy and detailed accuracy. These photographs should be read as poetic texts, carrying coded messages of value to all whose minds are open to the wisdom of the world. Their strength is in the outstanding features and highlights on which they dwell: a form of strength that mankind has inherited down the ages and that has enabled life to survive and spread. The dignity manifest in these photographs will encourage viewers to bring to the definition of the term "desert" such epithets as beautiful, mysterious, inviting, even salutary.

Herr Martin's intention is to bring Africa in its true colours before the Western eye and mind. If Western observers begin to understand that aspect of the deserts of Africa, they will confirm the aims of this book, and at the same time participate in a joyful tribute to an area and a culture that hold many of the great secrets of existence.

An appreciation of those secrets has been lost in the world of today, and consequently the desert has come to be regarded as a place of absence. The pages that follow will show very clearly that the desert means presence: the presence of life, of culture and of power. The only barren deserts that threaten to annihilate human values are those that lie within us. Such deserts as these devour the human spirit, leave the psyche parched, and place us in the dangerous situation of people without roots in the world of the spirit. The yearning of so many in the west for spiritual meaning, their sense of homelessness and loss amidst all the material plenty of their lives, illustrate the urgent need to reconcile the inner and the outer world. The photographs here may be seen as an important step in that direction; after all, there is a direct connection between natural and spiritual deserts. As we shall see here, natural deserts are full of life, a proud life reflected in the eyes of those who have chosen to make their home there. Natural deserts guard spiritual riches and the way into another world, reaffirming beauty in the face of desolation.

Unlike these natural deserts, the desert of the spirit is lifeless and without dignity. It is painfully empty, and we are usually helpless to do anything about it, even though we long for its drought to be quenched some day by the inner rains of the spirit. Seen in this light, *The Deserts of Africa* is an oasis amidst the west's devastation of the spirit, and this book also aims to exercise a healing influence on human perception by showing that the bleak face of the natural wilderness conceals a resonant wealth of spiritual life.

The Deserts of Africa is an invaluable and committed contribution to the cause of cultural recovery; it sets out to relieve the drought of the Western mind and provide new strength in revealing the connection between natural deserts and the source of cultural values. This book shows that beauty can be present wherever the human mind receives spiritual nourishment: a revolutionary idea, and one calculated to encourage those who love Africa to maintain their connections with that ancient continent, an thereby reinforce their links with the world of the spirit.

In looking at these pictures, you will embark on a fascinating journey of the mind, leading to a place where all we had taken for granted is shaken by an irresistible call to return to our spiritual roots.

Malidoma and Sobonfu Somé
Burkina Faso, 1998

The inhabitants of the oasis of Séguédine are Kanuri people. Only a few of the oasis children have an opportunity to attend the state-run school.

الله أكبَر

Over millions of years, erosion has carved the
western rim of the Djado plateau into huge cones
and blocks of rock.

THE SAHARA

A sea without water

The Sahara is the desert *par excellence*, larger and more
extreme in climate than the Namib, Atacama or Gobi deserts.
It stretches over 4,000 miles, from the Atlantic in the west to
the Red Sea in the east, and extends over 15 degrees of latitude
from the Atlas Mountains in the north down to black Africa.
With a surface area of 3.5 million square miles, it is larger than
Europe or the USA – geographers sometimes call it the
"desert continent".

To this day, the Sahara is a forbidding barrier between Europe
and black Africa. There is still no trans-Saharan highway, and
even the two major north–south tracks have been impassable
(except to local traffic) for years because the risks of keeping
them open are too great. For a very long time, exploration of the
Sahara was a dangerous undertaking. Few had the endurance
and good fortune of such 19th-century travellers as Heinrich
Barth who eventually reached the goal of their journey in the
bahr bela ma, the waterless sea, as the Sahara was called
by Arab caravan drivers.

The causes of the extreme drought and heat of the Sahara
are not, as with other deserts, to be sought in mountain ranges
that keep the rains away or in its distance from the ocean
or in cold sea currents, but are solely the result of the climatic
conditions of the tropics. Warm masses of air, carrying
a great deal of water, rise above the equator, cooling off as
they do so, and shed the water as rain over the equator itself.
To the north and south, above the tropics, the now dry masses
of air sink again and heat up. They then stream back into the
equatorial troughs of low pressure in the form of very dry
trade winds blowing close to the ground. The Sahara is thus
a typical tropical desert with an extreme climate. In many

The Tuareg salt caravan passing through the
Ténéré desert is called a *tarhalamt*. It is one of
the last salt caravans of the Sahara.

places, humidity is as low as five per cent, and in summer temperatures climb to values of 55 °C in the shade. As a result of the lack of cloud cover and vegetation, the difference between day and night temperatures is higher here than anywhere else on earth.

Geologically, the Sahara divides into nine great basins containing marine and continental deposits several thousand metres deep. Those deposits are of great economic importance today, since they contain not only extensive supplies of groundwater but also huge amounts of oil and natural gas. The great salt deposits of the Sahara are also located here. The sunken basins face curving rises of ground that are particularly conspicuous in the Central Sahara, and were formed by volcanic action in geologically recent times. The process created the Saharan ranges of the Hoggar, Aïr and Tibesti mountains, and the Adrar des Iforas, Djado and Ennedi high plateaux.

The transitional area from the Saharan basins to the rising ground is marked by the landscape areas known as Tassili – eroded sandstone plateaus –, among the most beautiful places in the Sahara because of the bizarre shapes to which they have weathered.

To this day, the word "Sahara" is a magically evocative term, conjuring up the image of endless seas of sand to the European mind. Yet only a fifth of the Sahara is actually sand, and only one-tenth of it is covered with dunes. In fact the Sahara consists of many entirely different landscapes to a greater degree than almost any other large natural expanse on earth; consider, for instance, the contrast between the Tibesti mountain range and the Ténéré desert that lies on its western border.

At its western rim the Djado plateau falls steeply to the sandy Ténéré desert. Here the desert sands blow around the rocks of Orida.

The Tibesti mountains are the most remote and inaccessible range in Africa. Volcanic activity, still in progress, has made them the highest mountains of the Sahara, and among the largest craters anywhere on earth, such as that of Emi Koussi, a well-known landmark in south-eastern Tibesti. The Trou au Natron, created by a powerful eruption, lies on the southern flank of the volcano of Pic Toussidé, 10,710 feet above sea level. New volcanoes quickly rose from the bottom of this crater, which is four miles in diameter and over half a mile deep; 15,000 years ago it was still filled by a lake 1,640 feet deep. Today, salt marshes cover part of the bottom of the crater.

The mountainous ramparts of the Tibesti, a range with over a dozen peaks 10,000 feet high, are at the mercy of the incessant north-east trade wind. Over millions of years, the sand abraded from the mountains has accumulated in the lee of the Tibesti, creating the Erg de Bilma, part of the 155,000 square miles of the Ténéré desert. Many lines of dunes can be traced almost unbroken from the Tibesti range to the Aïr mountains 500 miles further west.

While the Erg de Bilma conveys a sense of order and harmony, the desert in the plains of the Ténéré du Tafessasset to the north has reached its extreme phase of development. Animal and plant life seem non-existent, so that there is a sense of unreality about the New Stone Age grinding mortars, hand-axes and stone hatchets that have lain undisturbed in the sand for thousands of years. When Europe was submerged beneath a sheet of ice, climatic conditions in the Sahara were those of the Mediterranean today. Giraffes, buffalo and elephants grazed the tree-grown savannahs, and the New Stone Age hunter-gatherers portrayed them as the subjects of their rock art,

Kanuri people live in the oasis of Aney on the outskirts of the Ténéré desert, making a living from the yield of their date palms and the nearby saltworks. Their houses are built from sun-dried bricks of saline mud.

The rim of the Djado plateau.

making the Sahara the biggest open-air museum in the world. Even before the end of the Stone Age, permanent changes in the climate saw the decline of these cultures and turned the Sahara into the largest desert on earth.

The vegetation of the Sahara is notable for being particularly poor in species. There are only 1,400 plant species in an area of 3.5 million square miles – a figure that is reached in tropical rain forests in an area of only a few square miles. The reason lies in the harsh environmental conditions. The water supply is the crucial factor restricting life in the Sahara. While herbaceous plants and grasses try to get as much as possible of the very occasional rainfall by developing a spreading root system that stays close to the surface, trees usually have roots going deep down to reach the strata where there is groundwater. Many acacias have roots to a depth of 130 feet. However, the tree most frequently found in the Sahara is the tamarisk, which can even make use of salt water.

The same applies to the animal kingdom: its opportunities to develop are limited by the extreme shortage of water, which makes it all the more surprising that 50 species of mammals, 18 species of birds, 13 snake species and 17 scorpion species live in the Sahara, not to mention 350 species of black beetles. Most of the animal and plant species have adapted extremely well to their desert environment, as the camel (strictly speaking, the dromedary) makes impressively clear. Long legs raise its body high above the hot air close to the ground, its back, turned to the sun, is insulated by a thick layer of fat, while its flanks and belly carry almost no fat at all and thus give off heat. The animal's body temperature can rise to 46 °C before it comes to any harm. Its large hoofs prevent it from sinking into the sand.

The camel will tolerate water from salty springs, and can manage without drinking at all for weeks on end in winter.

Mankind, on the other hand, has no way of adapting physiologically to conditions in the desert, and can survive there only by perfect cultural adaptation. The Tubu people, for example, have adapted extremely well to the inhospitable conditions of the Tibesti mountains. It is said that a Tubu can live on a single date for three days. On the first day he eats the skin of the date, on the second day he eats the flesh of the fruit, and on the third day he eats the date stone. The Tubu graze their herds of goats on scree slopes where the human eye cannot see a blade of grass. The oasis gardens of Bardai and Yebbi Bou provide a certain amount of fruit and vegetables. Vital foodstuffs such as sugar, tea and grain are exchanged for dates, and caravans export salt and livestock to the Sahel and Fezzan.

The population of the Sahara consists of Berbers, Arabs, Jews and negroid peoples, although the Saharan Jews have almost all left the area in the last few decades. While the Tubu, Daza and Kanuri are among the negroid peoples of the Sahara, the Tuareg are Berbers. The Moors living in the western Sahara are sometimes classed with the Saharan Arabs, sometimes with the Berbers. Although the settlement areas of these Saharan peoples often overlap, mixed marriages are still extremely unusual.

About two and a half million people in all live in the Sahara, the majority of them in the oases. However, there are still hundreds of thousands of nomads in the area. In the valleys of the Ennedi, Tibesti, Aïr and Adrar des Iforas, and on the southern outskirts of the Sahara, a nomadic life is the only possible means of survival.

A Tubu from the oasis of Bilma passes through the Ténéré with his camels and goats. He is on a pilgrimage to the distant city of Mecca.

Probably the best-known of the Sahara peoples are the Tuareg, who also live in Algeria, Libya, Niger, Mali and Burkina Faso. Even today, however, nationality is not so important to the Tuareg as membership of their own confederations, for instance the confederations of the Kel Ahaggar, Kel Air or Kel Adrar. Tuareg is probably an Arabic loan word, meaning "those cast out by God". The singular form is Targi for men, Targia for women, and the Tuareg call themselves Imohar in the north and Imasheren in the south, both terms meaning "the free people". The Tuareg religion is Islamic, although most of them have only a sketchy acquaintance with the Koran, and the socially strong position of Tuareg women in particular is often out of line with its teachings.

Tuareg society has a clearly hierarchical structure. The Imasheren are at the top, and are often described as noblemen. In the past, their political and economic power derived from raiding expeditions and the tribute paid by their dependants. These, called the Imrad, are the largest class of society. Since their main occupation is rearing goats, they are also called Kel Ulli (goat people). The prestigious but economically less important business of breeding camels is reserved for the Imasheren. The Ineslemen are higher in the social scale than the Imrad, and are regarded as free, since they never owed tribute to the Imasheren. They are the scholars among the Tuareg, and concern themselves exclusively with religious questions. The dark-skinned Iklan, once slaves, are of low social standing, although economically they are often better off today than their former masters. The Enaden occupy a special position in Tuareg society: as smiths and craftsmen they are low in status, but their skills are needed for transactions with the outside world, and in circumcising young men.

Morning sunlight falls on the sandstone rocks of the Djado plateau.

As with other Saharan peoples, herds of camels and goats –
and also of sheep and cattle in the transitional southern area of
the Sahel – traditionally represent the most important factor in
the Tuareg economy. Oasis areas are cultivated where natural
conditions allow, but work in the oasis gardens is almost entirely
the province of the Iklan.

The caravan trade has done a great deal to build up the
mystique around the Tuareg as "knights of the desert". It is the
third pillar of the economy, especially for the Kel Ewey Tuareg of
the Aïr mountains. Their salt caravans, called *tarhalamt*, are the
only salt caravans of the Sahara still fully functional today. The
caravan season begins in autumn; the Tuareg camels are strong
by the end of the rainy season, and provisions of fodder can be
laid in. The caravans assemble in the nomad camps of the Aïr.
The camels, their loads and their companions are in the care of
the Madugu whose business it is to escort them safely through
the Ténéré desert – 250 of the 400 miles between the Aïr
mountains and Kaouar pass through the Ténéré. A caravan
will try to reach the few springs by making forced marches of
16 to 18 hours a day. Since there are almost no landmarks in
the Ténéré, the Madugu take their bearings by the position of
the sun, the structure of the sand, and the faint tracks left by
previous caravans. Fodder is left at regular intervals, and must
be found again on the way back. The inhabitants of the Kaouar
oases, most of them Kanuri, wait impatiently for the arrival of
the first caravans, since they rely on the millet and cones of
sugar brought by the Tuareg, who exchange them for the two
most important oasis products, salt and dates. The salt is won
in summer in the saltworks, in a very labour-intensive process,
and is now ready in large cones called *kantu* and smaller blocks

A Targia (Tuareg woman) in the oasis of Timia in the
Aïr mountains.

called *foshi*. After the conclusion of business, the caravan faces an even more strenuous journey back. Already weakened by the long journey out, the camels now have to carry 300 to 450 pounds of salt each, and their strength is often almost exhausted by the time they reach the first life-giving pastures of the Aïr mountains. But this is only the first part of the caravan season; salt and dates now have to be traded at a profit. There is particularly large demand for these goods in Hausa country – the south of Niger and northern Nigeria. Bilma salt in particular has a high reputation as salt for cattle and for culinary use, and can be sold or exchanged for ten times its purchase price. The Tuareg therefore very soon set out south to offer their wares in the markets of the Sahel, where they stock up not only with trade goods for the next *tarhalamt* but also with green tea (a popular drink), fabrics and household necessities. The Tuareg then wait in the pastures of Hausa country for their camel foals to be born before returning to their families in the Aïr mountains shortly before the beginning of the rainy season, and once they are home preparations for the next *tarhalamt* soon begin again.

It is difficult to estimate how many of the Tuareg, who number about a million in all, still lead the traditional nomadic life. Three events have had a major effect on them in recent decades. When French colonial rule came to an end in the early 1960s, the Tuareg were suddenly faced with an entirely different set of political circumstances. The new independent states were now ruled from their capitals by men who, as members of black African peoples, regarded the Tuareg with suspicion or hostility. Conflicts already centuries old broke out again between sedentary and nomadic peoples, the former slave owners and the enslaved.

Tuareg nomad children bathing in a *guelta* in the Adrar des Iforas. *Gueltas* are natural rock basins in which water is often held for months after rain has fallen.

Then, in 1973 and 1974, wide areas of the Sahel suffered
a terrible drought. The Tuareg lost all their cattle. Tens of
thousands of the people starved, since international aid was
requested much too late. Hundreds of thousands took refuge
in camps or in the few towns of the area, trying to scrape a living
as night watchmen or day labourers. The cattle herds were built
up again in the 1980s, but only a percentage of the Tuareg
returned to the old nomadic life, many thousands staying in
the refugee camps of southern Algeria. Their return to Mali and
Niger was organized in 1990 by the United Nations and the
International Committee of the Red Cross. However, much of
the material sent as aid was misappropriated, and as a result
there were Tuareg protest demonstrations, brutally suppressed
by the local troops. Thereupon the Tuareg revolted and struck
back with the utmost brutality themselves. Tuareg attacks on
military convoys and police stations brought retaliation in the
shape of massacres of the Tuareg civilian population. It was
soon obvious that this was a conflict which neither side could
win. Peace negotiations were hampered by the weakness
of governments in danger of being overthrown, and by
disagreements among the Tuareg themselves, which split the
Tuareg rebellion into many different factions. Eventually, the
Tuareg managed to get agreement to many of their demands
for greater justice and a certain degree of autonomy, and the
rebellion gradually died down in the year 1996. However, their
living conditions have not really improved much since then.

Most of the Tuareg live not in the Sahara but in the Sahel,
on the southern outskirts of the desert. The Sahel, a strip of land
on average 250 miles in breadth, extends from the Atlantic in
the west to the coast of Eritrea on the Red Sea in the east,

The salt caravan, or *tarhalamt*, of the Kel Ewey
Tuareg crosses the Ténéré desert in the
winter months.

4,000 miles away. For the trans-Saharan caravans of the past, returning from weeks among endless seas of sand to regions that were richer in vegetation, the Arabic term *Sahel* still had its original meaning of a shore or bank. Today, the Sahel zone has become synonymous with drought and hunger. The summer rains have failed again and again since the early 1970s, and drought has led to catastrophic famines costing millions of human lives.

The climate is determined by the long dry seasons and the short rainy season, which lasts from May to October in the southern Sahel, but is much shorter further north. The amount of precipitation varies a great deal, and in many years there is none at all. Since time immemorial the Sahel has been regularly plagued by drought, but only in recent decades have these droughts caused such devastating famines. The reason may be sought in the kind of human interference with the eco-system that has led to the expansion of deserts – a phenomenon described as desertification. The herds of the Tuareg, Bororo and Moors, which are often larger than they used to be, give the pastures no chance to regenerate. Once the grass has been completely destroyed, trees are felled so that the animals can eat their leaves, and countless trees have also been sacrificed to the need for firewood, since wood is the only available source of energy in this area. Such conduct, understandable from the point of view of the nomads but inappropriate to the sensitive eco-system of the Sahel, weakens the vegetation so much that it dies entirely in periods of drought, leaving the land at the mercy of the sun and wind. Islands of desert form, particularly around villages and springs, and extend constantly, merging into large expanses of desert. The only way of countering this

The Marble Mountains rise from the sandy Ténéré desert like islands in the sea of time.

development is to reduce the size of the herds and observe strictly controlled rotation of grazing, so that the affected pasture areas can regenerate. Some way must also be found to reduce the rapidly increasing birth rate, which will inevitably lead to greater and greater over-exploitation of natural resources.

In this situation, it is easy to forget that cities like Timbuktu, Oualata and Gao were once centres of international culture, impressively contradicting the idea, still current, that Africa is a continent without a history. It is thought that explorers from the kingdom of Mali, which gave the present state its name, almost discovered America 200 years before Columbus. The mission of the fleet sent out by King Abubakari II around 1300 was to sail west until it came to new shores. None of the ships came home. A more successful expedition was King Kankan Musa's pilgrimage to Mecca in the 14th century, unequalled to this day. The monarch travelled with his court and a retinue of 60,000 men. Five hundred slaves carried the gold he took with him, and he distributed 20,000 gold pieces as alms when he reached Mecca. It was twelve years before the gold market recovered from this assault on it.

Today the Sahel states of Chad, Niger, Mali and Mauritania are among the poorest states on earth. Corrupt governments, the absence of almost any kind of infrastructure, difficult agricultural conditions, and a high birth rate are only a few of the many reasons that have so far prevented any profitable long-term development of the Sahel areas. Even extensive development aid has had very little in the way of lasting success to its credit in the last few decades.

The farmers and nomads of the Sahel know they can expect no support from the state. The strength and dignity with which these people conduct their daily lives is all the more impressive in the light of this fact.

A Bororo nomad in Agadez. The Bororo are nomadic cattle breeders who travel around the Niger area with their herds.

The Wau en Namus lies in the middle of the monotonous stony deserts of southern Libya. The crater was created when the heart of a volcano erupted. A new volcano formed in the crater, surrounded by lakes fed by the groundwater.

The Mandara lakes lie in the sea of sand that is
the Libyan Erg Ubari. There are 15 lakes, fed by
groundwater thousands of years old.

The Trou au Natron in the Tibesti mountains of
Chad was created by a huge volcanic eruption.
Small younger volcanoes rose from the bottom of
the crater. The Trou au Natron is over half a mile
deep, and has a diameter of four miles.

ⵙⵜⵏⵏⵉⵍⵏⵉⵜⵏⵏ ⵎⵙⵙⵙⵙⵎ ⵉ ⵙⵏⵉⵉⵙ
ⵙ ⵙⵏⵜⵙⵎⴰ ⵉⵏⵜ ⵙⵙⵙⵏⵙⵎⵄ ⵜⵙⵙ

The dunes of Temet lie on the eastern outskirts of
the Aïr mountains. At 1,000 feet, they are among
the highest dunes in the Sahara.

Temet is the name given by the Tuareg to an area
on the eastern outskirts of the Aïr mountains,
where the north-east trade wind has piled the sand
of the Ténéré desert in front of the mountain range.

The veil worn by Tuareg men is more than a
protection from sun and dust. Its colour and quality
provide information about the wearer's regional
and social origin.

The Blue Mountains (also known as the Marble Mountains) seem to be drowning in the sandy sea of the Ténéré desert. They consist of marble which glows blue when seen in a certain light.

When Europe was submerged beneath a sheet of
ice, the Sahara had a Mediterranean climate. Rock
art and grinding mortars are evidence of New
Stone Age culture. The mortar opposite is lying on
the completely flat plain of the Ténéré desert. The
rock drawing is in the Tassili n'Ajjer.

The sandstone rocks of Orida, on the western rim
of the Djado plateau, fall steeply to the Ténéré.

ⵛⵉⵏⵏⵗⵛⵉⵏⵗⵛⵗⵉⵏ
ⵜⵏⵏⵗⵜ⵿⵿ⵏⵉⵜⵖⵙⵛⵉⵜ
ⵠⵙⵉⵏ꞉ⵗⵉⵏⵗⴴⴴ꞉ⵉⵜ
ⵛⵉⵏⵗⵜⵏⵉ꞉
⸱⸱⸱ⵣⵉⵠ꞉ⵜⵠⵉⵜ
⸱⸱⸱ⵛⵉⵠ꞉ⵜⵉⵏⵗ꞉
ⵔⵖⴳⵉⵏ꞉ⵉⵜ

Tuareg women are not veiled. Although the Tuareg are Muslims, women occupy an honoured position in their society.

اللهُ أَكبَر   اللهُ أَكبَر

اللّهُ أَكبَر   اللّهُ أَكبَر

أَشهَدُ أَن لا إلهَ إلّا اللّه   أَشهَدُ أَن لا إلهَ إلّا اللّه

أَشهَدُ أَنَّ مُحَمَّدًا رَسُولُ اللّه   أَشهَدُ أَنَّ مُحَمَّدًا رَسُولُ اللّه

حَيَّ عَلَى الصَّلاة   حَيَّ عَلَى الصَّلاة

حَيَّ عَلَى الفَلَاح   حَيَّ عَلَى الفَلَاح

اللّهُ أَكبَر   اللّهُ أَكبَر

لا إلهَ إلّا اللّه

A representative of the sultan keeps watch over the mosque in Agadez. The minaret of this mosque is among the best-known buildings in Africa, and has become a famous landmark of Agadez. It is constructed of clay in the Sudanese style of building.

Tuareg, Tubu, Arabs, Bororo and Hausa may all be
encountered in the camel market of Agadez. These
very different peoples communicate in the Hausa
trade language.

The Bororo, nomadic stockbreeders, live in the western Sahel. They own huge herds of cattle, but also keep camels to ride and as beasts of burden.

ⵏⵉⴶⵜⵜⵏⵉⵉⵛⵏⵝⵜⵛⴰⵏⵣⵏⵉⵏⵥⵥⵜⵉⵔ

Trading begins in the camel market of Agadez at first light of dawn. The famous white riding camels of the Tuareg fetch the highest prices.

Girls make expeditions lasting several days
to collect firewood for the oasis of Aney on the
edge of the Ténéré desert. Finding firewood and
preparing food is the task of women and girls.

بسم الله الرحمن الرحيم

يَـٰٓأَيُّهَا ٱلَّذِينَ ءَامَنُوا۟ كُتِبَ عَلَيْكُمُ ٱلصِّيَامُ كَمَا
كُتِبَ عَلَى ٱلَّذِينَ مِن قَبْلِكُمْ لَعَلَّكُمْ تَتَّقُونَ ۝
أَيَّامًا مَّعْدُودَٰتٍ ۚ فَمَن كَانَ مِنكُم مَّرِيضًا أَوْ عَلَىٰ سَفَرٍ
فَعِدَّةٌ مِّنْ أَيَّامٍ أُخَرَ ۚ وَعَلَى ٱلَّذِينَ يُطِيقُونَهُۥ فِدْيَةٌ طَعَامُ
مِسْكِينٍ ۖ فَمَن تَطَوَّعَ خَيْرًا فَهُوَ خَيْرٌ لَّهُۥ ۚ وَأَن تَصُومُوا۟
خَيْرٌ لَّكُمْ ۖ إِن كُنتُمْ تَعْلَمُونَ ۝ شَهْرُ رَمَضَانَ ٱلَّذِىٓ أُنزِلَ فِيهِ
ٱلْقُرْءَانُ هُدًى لِّلنَّاسِ وَبَيِّنَٰتٍ مِّنَ ٱلْهُدَىٰ وَٱلْفُرْقَانِ ۚ فَمَن
شَهِدَ مِنكُمُ ٱلشَّهْرَ فَلْيَصُمْهُ ۖ وَمَن كَانَ مَرِيضًا أَوْ عَلَىٰ سَفَرٍ فَعِدَّةٌ
مِّنْ أَيَّامٍ أُخَرَ ۗ يُرِيدُ ٱللَّهُ بِكُمُ ٱلْيُسْرَ وَلَا يُرِيدُ بِكُمُ ٱلْعُسْرَ وَلِتُكْمِلُوا۟
ٱلْعِدَّةَ وَلِتُكَبِّرُوا۟ ٱللَّهَ عَلَىٰ مَا هَدَىٰكُمْ وَلَعَلَّكُمْ تَشْكُرُونَ ۝

صدق الله العظيم

Timbuktu's largest mosque, the Djinger-Ber, was built by King Kankan Musa of Mali in the 14th century. The pilgrimage of Kankan Musa has gone down in history. He gave away so much gold on this expedition that it took the world gold market twelve years to recover.

After the decline of Timbuktu, the little oasis of
Oualata in the south-east of Mauritania became a
centre of Islamic scholarship. The walls of Oualata,
ornamented with geometrical patterns, have,
since the 15th century, housed the largest libraries
in the western Sahara.

The volcanic island of Guinni Koma lies just off the shores of Djibouti. Nowhere else in the Rift Valley is it more obvious that two continental plates are drifting apart than at this point on the earth's crust.

THE RIFT VALLEY
Land of the nomads

The Rift Valley is a fault trough about 4,000 miles long, extending from the valley of the Jordan in Israel across the Red Sea, through Ethiopia and East Africa, and down to Mozambique. For 18 million years, two continental plates have been drifting apart at a speed of up to an inch a year at this point on the earth's crust, turning the Red Sea into a new ocean. The process of ocean formation is only just beginning in Ethiopia and East Africa, but here too the earth's crust has already stretched enough to form a depression up to 2,000 feet deep, enabling magma to rise through cracks in the crust, a phenomenon which explains the constant volcanic activity in the Rift Valley.

The deserts of the Rift Valley are not large by comparison with the Sahara, but are equally hostile to human life. Their names are hardly known in Europe: they are the Danakil, Chalbi and Kaisut deserts. There are two reasons for the lack of precipitation in these areas. First, the Rift Valley, like the whole of East Africa, lies in the region affected by the north-east trade wind, which brings hot, dry masses of air from the Arabian peninsula to displace the damp equatorial air. The strong relief of the Rift Valley, however, leads to an unusually pronounced difference in the amounts of rainfall it receives. The mountainous peripheral areas, the volcanoes, and the highlands on the floor of the fault trough receive plenty of rain, and with their volcanic soil they are among the richest agricultural regions of the entire African continent. In contrast to these areas, there are deserts and semi-deserts on the lee side of the mountain ranges, where little rain falls.

The Rift Valley has three different areas of desert or semi-desert: the Danakil desert beside the Red Sea, the desert-like

Nomadic Somali woman in Marsabit. The women come to the market of Marsabit to offer cheese and leather goods for sale.

north of Kenya, and the soda deserts of Lake Magadi and
Lake Natron on the borders of Kenya and Tanzania.

The largest desert in the Rift Valley is the Danakil desert
in the Afar triangle. Its north-east border is the Eritrean coast
of the Red Sea between Massawa and Aseb, and to the west
it is bordered by the steep rise of the Ethiopian highlands,
into which it projects southward like a wedge. Its core area
is the Danakil valley, which is up to 400 feet below sea level
and is one of the hottest and most inhospitable places
on earth. The course of the Rift Valley is marked here by
a great many active volcanoes, hot springs and salt lakes.
Hundreds of geysers send up jets of steam and highly
concentrated salt solutions. When the boiling water cools
down, the minerals crystallize, forming yellowish green
battlements and ramparts. The Danakil valley used to be
subject to repeated flooding by the Red Sea, the last occasion
being 10,000 years ago. After that, lava streams blocked off
the flooded valley and the salt water it contained evaporated,
leaving a layer of salt 6,500 feet deep created by the
successive floods of seawater. Even today, caravans from
the highlands of Ethiopia come down to the valley to fetch
salt, which has been broken from the banks of the saltwater
Lake Asale by Afar nomads for centuries. About 100,000 Afar
nomads live in the Danakil desert and are usually described
in books on the area as "savage and cruel", a prejudice
probably fostered not least by the fact that the Afar used to
cut off their enemies' testicles and hang them around their own
necks as trophies. In all, 750,000 Afar live today in Ethiopia,
Eritrea and Djibouti, the former French colony of the "Territory
of the Afar and Issa".

Afar nomads in the Danakil desert, which runs
parallel to the coast of the Red Sea and is one of
the hottest places on earth.

During the 30-year war of liberation in Eritrea, the Afar formed a resistance group of their own – the Afar Liberation Front – led by Sultan Ali Mirah. Even after the fall of the Mengistu regime in Ethiopia, parts of the Liberation Front remained active, and they still make journeys through the Danakil valley, a dangerous undertaking.

South of the Danakil desert, the Rift Valley narrows to a trough barely 30 miles broad, rising to the highlands of Ethiopia and reaching a height of 6,000 feet to the south. Its course is marked by a chain of lakes. Between the highlands of southern Ethiopia and the fertile uplands of central and western Kenya there is a desert-like area in northern Kenya. With a surface area of 115,000 square miles, it occupies over half of the country. The relief shows little variation: it is a gently rolling plateau of semi-desert from which occasional volcanic mountain ranges emerge. Because of their exposed position, they receive good amounts of rainfall. The volcano of Mount Marsabit, 6,120 feet high, with the dense and misty forests on its slopes and large herds of elephants, lies to the east of the Chalbi and Kaisut deserts. The Rift Valley does not follow as strikingly linear a course here as in central Kenya; its clearest marking is indicated by Lake Turkana, which fills the northern part of the Kenyan Rift Valley.

Northern Kenya is nomad country: 79,000 Boran live between the Ethiopian border and Marsabit, 30,000 Gabbra between Marsabit and the eastern banks of Lake Turkana, and the Samburu live further to the south. Their neighbours are the Rendille, who share a similar culture. West of Lake Turkana is the country inhabited by Turkana nomads, who still raid the Pokot and Samburu regions on their southern borders.

Boran nomad child in a sandstorm on the edge of the Chalbi desert.

In accordance with their different environments the Samburu, Pokot, Turkana and Boran people raise cattle, and the Rendille and Gabbra breed camels, but the deterioration of natural resources has made many cattle breeders turn to raising camels as well in recent years. Cattle raiding is still customary today, despite all attempts by the police and the army to abolish the practice.

During the colonial period the peoples of northern Kenya were largely left to their own devices. The interests of the British colonial power concentrated on the great agricultural potential of the Kenyan highlands. In the 1970s the Kenyan government began its attempts to better integrate the huge northern part of the country into the state. To mitigate the effects of recurrent droughts, centres for food distribution were set up and deep wells were bored. In the long term, both measures had catastrophic ecological consequences: the provision of food aid, continued beyond the actual periods of drought, and the growing number of mission stations attracted nomads even from very distant regions. They had lost their cattle during the drought, and are often still living in what should have been temporary settlements. Meanwhile, those who still have cattle or have acquired new herds graze them close to these stations, where there are deep wells guaranteeing a reliable water supply. However, the soil is too poor to bear such a burden. It is useless to make ecologically sensible demands for a reduction in the size of cattle herds, since from the nomads' point of view the larger their herds, the greater the chance of some animals surviving to keep human families from starvation and to form the foundation stock for building up a new herd. Moreover, cattle occupy a very special position in the nomadic cultures of

Two blind men and a sighted man in the village of Maikona, on the edge of the Chalbi desert. They are sitting outside a small bar, as they have done every day for many years, participating in the public life of the village.

northern Kenya. They do not just represent a form of currency and a source of food: they are at the heart of the entire value system of the nomads, a phenomenon described as the "cattle complex".

As a result of the difficult political and economic situation of Kenya, the north of the country was ignored by the Moi regime during the 1990s, and security deteriorated even further. The convoy of heavy vehicles moving daily from Isiolo to Ethiopia by way of Marsabit has a military escort, but it regularly comes under fire from gangs of marauding Shifta from Somalia. Cattle raids, carried out with heavy weapons today, kill hundreds of people every year. In 1997 the Turkana drove thousands of Samburu from their pastures by armed force. Throughout the north of the country it is impossible to use many of the urgently needed areas of grazing for fear of hostile attacks. The integration of the north with the rest of the country, as proclaimed in Kenyan propaganda for years, has failed entirely. If a Boran or Gabbra travels to the capital, Nairobi, he or she still says that he or she is "going to Kenya".

In central Kenya, the Rift Valley cuts through fertile highlands. Again, its course is marked by a chain of lakes – Lake Baringo, Lake Bogoria, Lake Nakuru and Lake Naivasha. To the south, the floor of the valley drops by over 3,000 feet, and amounts of rainfall sink to desert values again. This is where the Maasai, semi-nomadic cattle breeders, live with their herds. On the border between Kenya and Tanzania, the course of the Rift Valley is marked by Lake Magadi and Lake Natron. Lake Magadi is not only the lowest-lying but also the hottest and most inhospitable place in Kenya. Its waters are full of soda on which thrives an algae that gives the surface a pink and white

Maasai children by Lake Natron in northern Tanzania. They are hoping that the storm clouds will bring the eagerly awaited rains.

shimmer. This water-soluble salt (sodium carbonate) forms from the evaporating water constantly bubbling up from underground springs. Soda serves as the raw material for glassmaking (phosphates), and is mined by the Magadi Soda Company. It is also used for fertiliser and is one of the country's most important exports.

South of Lake Magadi, and now on Tanzanian territory, lies Lake Natron. Here too soda reaches the lake from underground springs. Single-celled and purple algae tinge the lake with red in some areas. The rising soda forms huge white "eyes", and regular polygonal patterns that are visible only from the air.

The soda desert of Lake Natron is dominated by the heights of Ol-Doinyo Lengai, "The mountain of God", sacred to the Maasai. According to their mythology, it is the home of their god Enkai, who once let cattle down to the Maasai on earth by the roots of the wild fig tree. The circular crater of this volcano does indeed look as if it might be the throne of the gods. Liquid carboniferous lava, known as white lava, flows like black ink from conical formations as high as houses, cooling within hours to white, calcareous and crumbly stone. Ol-Doinyo Lengai is the unusual example of a cold volcano; at 500 °C, its lava is not hot enough to glow red.

To the south-west lie the green highlands of the gigantic craters. The best known of them is the Ngorongoro Crater south of the Olduvai Gorge where, in the 1960s, Louis and Mary Leakey found the bones of an early ancestor of mankind, 1.8 million years old. Other sites in the Rift Valley where fossils of hominids have been found, for instance at Koobi Fora near Lake Turkana, suggest that East Africa, and the Rift Valley in particular, was indeed the cradle of humanity.

View of the steep slopes of the Rift Valley, with the volcano Ol-Doinyo Lengai.

Dawn breaks over the little town of Wade in the
Eritrean part of the Danakil desert. Eritrean troops
are posted here to guard the nearby border with
Ethiopia. The border conflict between Ethiopia and
Eritrea has cost tens of thousands of lives, and has
been a severe setback to the development of both
countries.

The small state of Djibouti on the Red Sea is
inhabited by Afar and Issa peoples. The Afar men
carry a curved sword known as a *gille*, which they
used in the past to castrate and kill their enemies.
The woman above is an Issa.

The Samburu of northern Kenya are semi-nomadic cattle breeders, and are linguistically and culturally closely related to the Maasai who live further south.

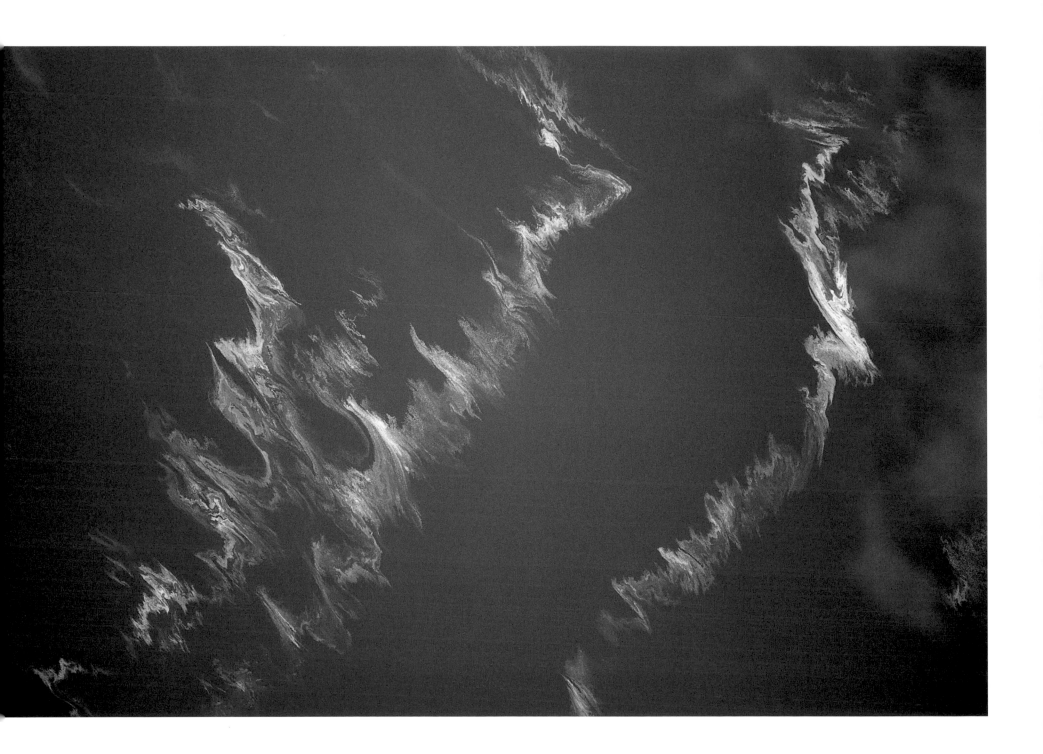

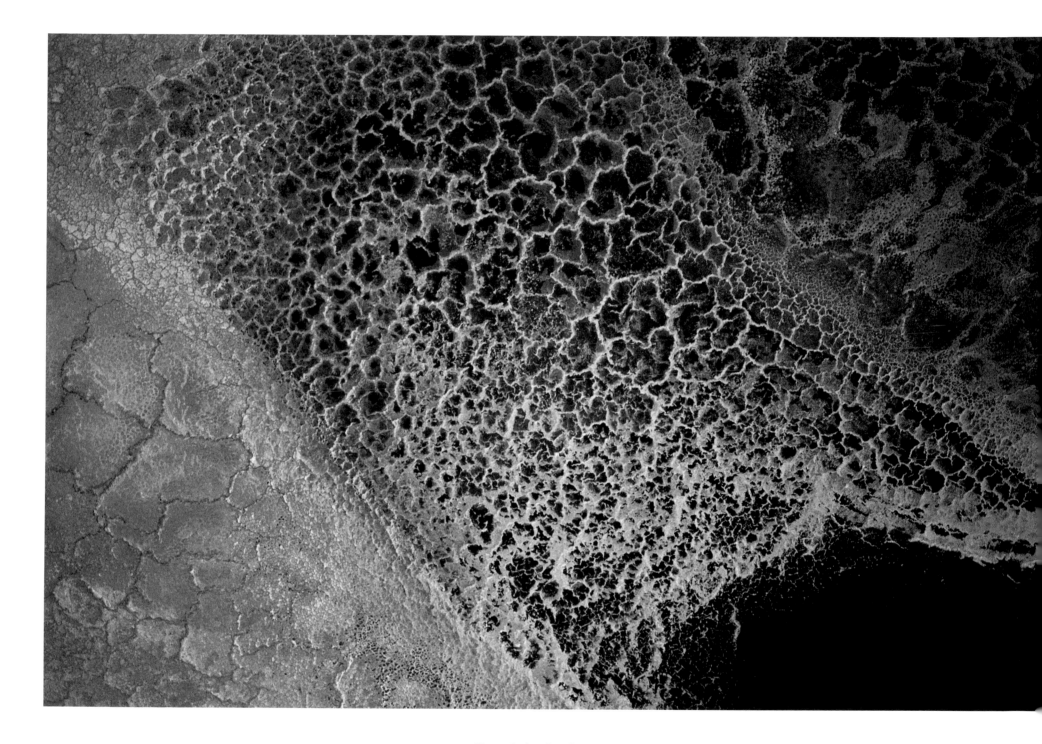

The soda that rises from underground springs drifts on the surface of Lake Natron, forming regular polygonal patterns where the water has dried up. The soda leaches out of the volcanic rock of the Rift Valley.

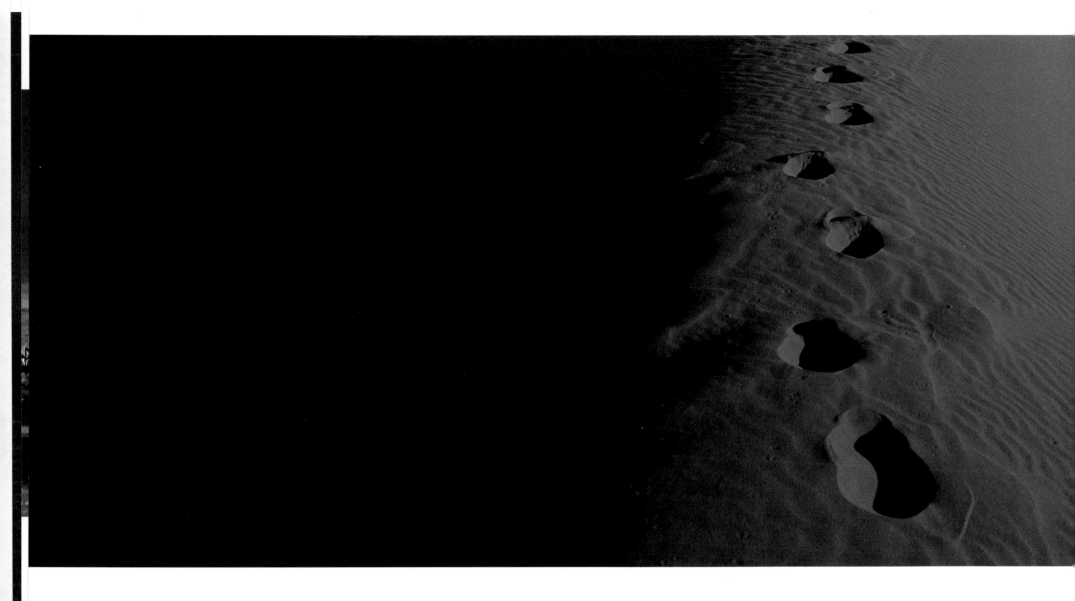

The Kalahari is the largest continuous expanse of sand in the world. The typical red colour is the result of oxidation processes.

THE KALAHARI
A journey to a lost world

However, the greatest density of animals in the Kalahari, and perhaps in the whole of Africa, is found in the Okavango delta. The Okavango river comes from the Benguela plateau in Angola, which gets plenty of rain. After leaving its source it has already flowed hundreds of miles through the Kalahari before it forms a huge inland delta 12 miles long; with an area of 10,000 miles, it is only slightly smaller than the Nile delta. The waters of the Okavango take five months to make their way from their entry into the delta through the sands of the Kalahari to the other side at Maun, flooding the delta itself. Lions, elephants, giraffes, antelopes and many other animal species of the African savannah live in close proximity on the islands of land that emerge from the water, as if on Noah's ark. However, this spectacle has become less frequent in recent decades. Poor rainy seasons in Angola, and the diversion of large quantities of water for irrigation projects in Namibia, have lowered the water level considerably, threatening the unique eco-system of the area. The realization of Namibian plans to ensure the water supply of the capital, Windhoek, by installing a gigantic pipeline has had a catastrophic effect on the delta.

Fifty years ago large parts of the Kalahari were still thought of as unexplored and inaccessible. Today, its great expanses are criss-crossed by a dense network of roads, tracks and cattle enclosures. Botswana was among the 20 poorest countries in the world when large deposits of diamonds were discovered in the Kalahari in 1967, and now the mines of Orapa, Jwaneng and Letlhakane make modern Botswana the largest diamond producer in the world. The most important branch of the economy, however, is cattle rearing on a large scale. Cattle owners with large amounts of capital behind them have recently

The Okavango river, originating in the mountains of Angola, flows through the sands of the Kalahari in the north-west of Botswana, creating the Okavango delta, famous for its wealth of wildlife.

penetrated further and further into the Kalahari, boring wells and opening up new pastures for the 80 million cattle in the area today. Massive over-grazing inevitably led to the degradation of large areas of the eco-system of the Kalahari.

The San people, on the other hand, have provided an impressive demonstration that it is possible to live in the Kalahari for thousands of years without destroying it. Their life-style, as hunters and gatherers, was in harmony with nature. They had a highly specialized understanding of their environment, they did not change it, they maintained the natural balance and they adapted to their environmental conditions.

To this day accounts of the lives of the San are found under the heading of "Bushmen". This term derives from the explorer Peter Kolb, who met the San in 1719 and called them "Buschjes Mannes", men of the bush, because their diet consisted of game, roots and honey. Anthropologists have tended to use the name "San", as they are called by the neighbouring Nama people. Recently, however, the Kalahari Bushmen have asked to be officially called "Bushmen" rather than "San" which they consider derogatory. They do not use any generic name among themselves. They used to live in small groups of 20 to 50 people next to a waterhole, and their dwellings consisted of semi-circular screens to protect them from the wind. As hunters, they knew 55 species of edible mammals, birds, reptiles and insects, and would cover up to 2,500 miles through the Kalahari in search of game during a single year. They used arrowheads made of bone or the horns of the oryx antelope, painted with deadly poison obtained from beetle larvae. However, their main source of nourishment was always the berries, roots, nuts and honey they gathered. Old women of the San people can still list over 100 edible plants in the

Sandy wind in the central Kalahari.

Kalahari. If the last waterholes ran dry in periods of drought, the San had ways of extracting water from baobab trees and wild melons. They also knew dry riverbeds where it was possible to siphon up several litres of water a day from the subsoil through a hollow stem of elephant grass. The San religion varies; in the southern San groups the praying mantis has divine status whilst others worship the sun as their highest deity.

Before the Bantu peoples confined themselves to the southern part of Africa in the last millennium, the San roamed not only the Kalahari but also the bordering highlands as far as the coast, leaving evidence of their presence in the many examples of rock art found in those areas. But not only did black farmers and cattle breeders displace the hunters over the course of centuries, white settlers from the south-west also flooded into their former territory. The San moved further and further into the Kalahari as the new arrivals came, waiting to see what would happen, and the final process of displacement began when parts of the territory that still remained theirs were declared nature reserves.

Baobab tree on Kubu Island. The baobab is often found in those parts of the Kalahari that receive most moisture.

In 1958 Sir Laurens van der Post published his fine book, *The Lost World of the Kalahari*, describing his months of searching for the last of the Bushmen who were still living the life of hunter-gatherers. Today, more than 40 years later, their culture has in effect been extinguished and their living space destroyed.

Most of the remaining 65,000 San now earn a living as farmhands, or survive without any prospects on the outskirts of towns and villages. Many can endure the loss of their identity only with the prop of alcohol. Theirs was a culture that survived in the Kalahari for thousands of years, and yet it took only a few decades to destroy it for ever.

Mokoro boats are made with curved axes by Tswana shepherds from hardwood trees; it takes weeks of work, but they are the main means of transport in the Okavango delta.

Today most of the San have few prospects, and live on the outskirts of towns and villages. Many can endure the loss of their identity only with the prop of alcohol. They were hunter-gatherers, and thus depended on an intact eco-system in the area where they roamed. The seizure of their land by white farmers and mining companies deprived them of their basis of existence, and now there are only 65,000 San left. The Maasai, regarded as traditionalists, are warlike and confident people, while the San were always very peaceful and reserved.

A San lights the morning fire in his hut. He earns a living for his family as a day labourer on a farm.

For centuries, the San roamed the Kalahari, living as hunters and gatherers. They carried their poisoned arrows in quivers made from the trunks of a tree known as the quiver tree.

San warming themselves by the fire in the chilly morning, in the village of Molapo in the central Kalahari.

The Kalahari has been opened up more and more rapidly in the last few decades by road-building, diamond mining, and the creation of cattle enclosures and national parks. The resultant change has deprived the San of their whole traditional way of life.

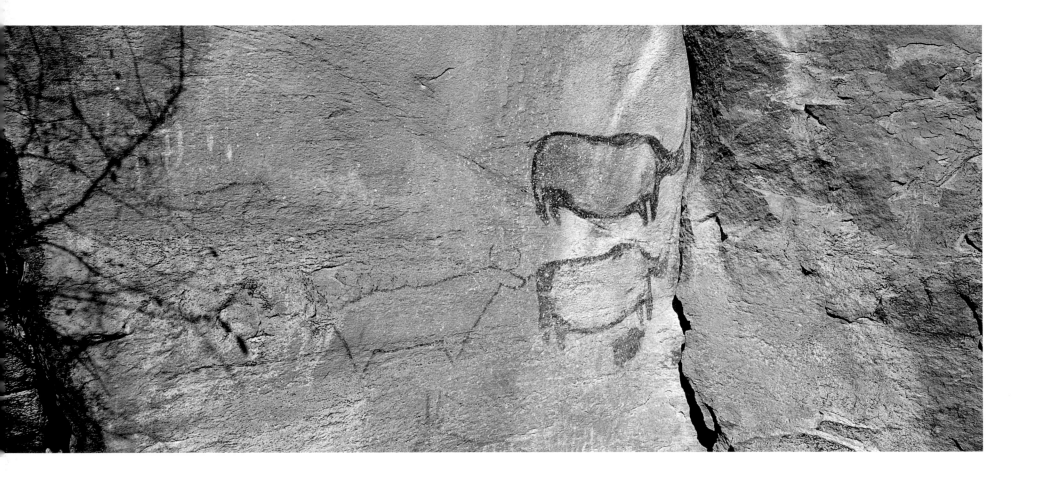

The rock art of the San is like a record in stone of a vanished culture. Today, San children offer bows and arrows for sale as souvenirs at service stations.

THE GODS MUST BE CRAZY

In 1980 the South African feature film *The Gods Must Be Crazy* was made in the Kalahari. The film tells the story of Xixo, who one day finds a Coca Cola bottle fallen from a plane in the middle of the Kalahari. Incredulous, he picks it up and takes it to his village. The bottle soon causes trouble and discord, and Xixo decides to take it back to the place where he found it. Through comedy, the film gives an impressive account of the gulf between the traditional life of the San and the modern world. The leading actor in the film, a San called Nixau, never recovered from the experience. Today, he lives with his family, forgotten, in a small village on the border between Namibia and Botswana.

The dunes of the Namib, up to 1,000 feet in height, divide the Atlantic coast from the agricultural land to the east, and are almost impassable to man and beast alike.

THE NAMIB
The oldest desert on earth

Compared to the Sahara, the Namib is only a small desert. It is 1,250 miles long, and has a surface area of only 54,000 square miles. The Orange River forms its southern border, and to the north the Namib extends to Angola. To the west it is bordered by the Atlantic, and to the east by the Great Rand, a belt of high plateau country that runs north to south through Namibia and separates the Namib desert from the Kalahari desert. From here the Namib falls in a sloping plane from a height of 26,000 feet to sea level. It was created in periods of drought that alternated with wetter periods, determining the climate of South Africa some three to four million years ago. The Namib is often described as the oldest desert on earth.

Because of its situation, the Namib belongs to the type of tropical deserts that encircle the earth like a girdle running around the northern and southern tropics. While the Sahara follows the northern tropic for 3,750 miles from the Atlantic to the Red Sea, the Namib extends only 30 to 90 miles from the Atlantic into the land mass of the African continent. The reason is to be sought in the great sea currents which affect the atmospheric circulation of South Africa, preventing the formation of a band of desert all the way from the Atlantic to the Indian Ocean. On the coast of the Indian Ocean, the warm Mozambique Stream provides adequate precipitation; on the Atlantic coast, in contrast, the Benguela Stream arrives from the Antarctic to reinforce the extreme drought of the tropic. As its icy waters well up they cause the damp, cool air masses over the Atlantic to shed all their rain before they reach the coast, and as a result the coastal strip of the Namib desert is one of the driest places on earth.

The climatic division of the Namib into the coastal Namib, the inner Namib and the outer Namib therefore follows the course of

Dunes of the Namib from the air.

considerable sense of self-worth. Cattle merchants now comb the Veld in motor vehicles, bartering sheep and goats with the Himba for alcohol. Almost every Himba kraal is now surrounded by empty bottles of cheap South African wine. An equally great threat comes from the meteoric rise in the tourist industry, which attempts to market the Kaukau Veld as an off-road adventure and the culture of the Himba as picturesque folklore.

However, the decline of the Himba would be final with the realization of the Epupa Dam project, which Angola and the Namibian regime would like to put into practice on the Kunene river on their joint border. The power station connected with the dam would be driven by a force of 300 to 500 megawatts, and development aid would meet the construction costs, equivalent to 225 million pounds sterling (360 million US dollars). Not only is the Kunene an important reserve to which the Himba can withdraw in times of drought, the flooding of the dam would also flood 150 of their sacred ancestral graves. Over and above the religious significance of these graves, they are also the key to Himba titles of land ownership. The more ancestors of previous generations are buried at a certain place, the stronger the present generation's claim to rights of residence and possession. This development will have a serious, if not disastrous, impact on the traditional life of the Himba. By making urgent representations, the Himba chief Kipuka has succeeded in getting his voice heard by the Namibian public in recent years, but recent African history has clearly shown that economic interests almost always prevail.

It is to be hoped that the "natural peoples" of Africa will be given some chance of adapting carefully to the accelerating pace of change in their environment, so that they can continue to lead a life of independence and dignity in this new millennium.

Herero woman in Sesfontein. The Herero, like other Africans, feel great respect for their old people, and consult them on all matters of importance. Different generations still tend to live together, and the small nuclear family is the exception rather than the rule.

Morning on the Spitzkoppe and evening in
the Dead Vlei. The mighty granite rocks of the
Spitzkoppe tower above the expanses of
Damaraland. It is among the highest mountains in
Namibia. The Dead Vlei is a mud pan above the
Sossus Vlei, and has not contained any water for
decades.

The Benguela Stream brings Antarctic waters to the coast of Namibia; there are even penguins on an island south of Lüderitz.

The Dead Vlei sees rainfall even more rarely than the Sossus Vlei, which lies slightly lower. The trees died here long ago. A dune now bars the way of the flash floods that very occasionally flow down the Tsauchab sand river to the Dead Vlei; this water is not from local rainfall, but is brought down the riverbed from areas of Namibia that receive more precipitation.

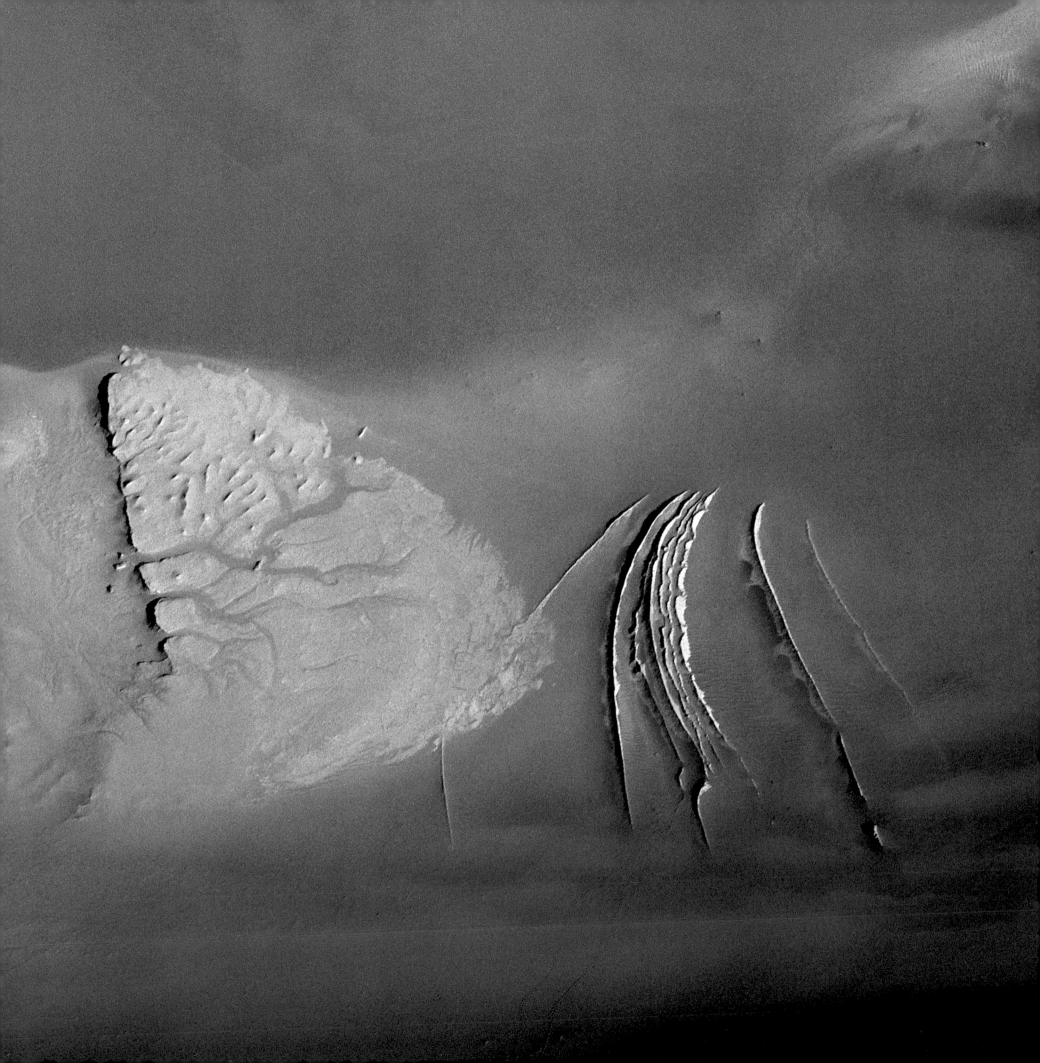

The wind, blowing alternately from the Atlantic and from the interior of the country, shapes the sand dunes of the Namib, which also line the course of the Tsauchab sand river. Water flows along the riverbed only a few times a century, but the groundwater level is high enough to be reached by the roots of isolated trees.

The largest and purest diamonds on earth are
found in the dunes of the Namib.

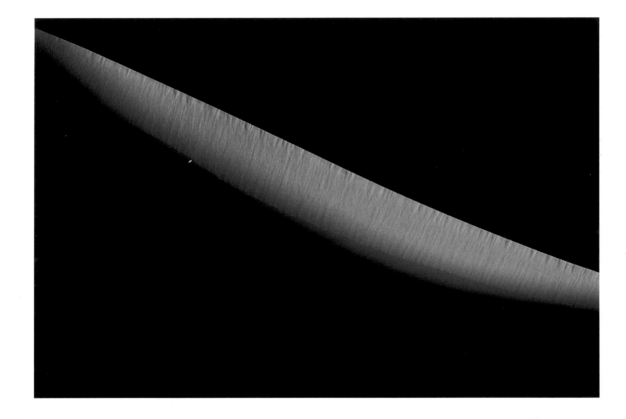

Dunes and dead trees line the course of the
Tsauchab sand river. Its bed very rarely contains
water, and it is even more unusual for flooding to
be sufficient to reach the Sossus Vlei in the middle
of the dunes.

In 1997 a rare miracle took place in the Namib. The bed of the Tsauchab sand river filled with water in a flash flood which reached the Sossus Vlei, suddenly creating a deep blue lake among the dunes.

A storm brewing over the Namib.

A termite mound at the foot of the Spitzkoppe, whose mighty granite rocks dominate the south of Damaraland. The Spitzkoppe was created by intrusion. About 200 million years ago, magma made its way into older rock strata. Wind and weather have carried the less resistant kinds of rocks away over millions of years, exposing the granite core of the mountain.

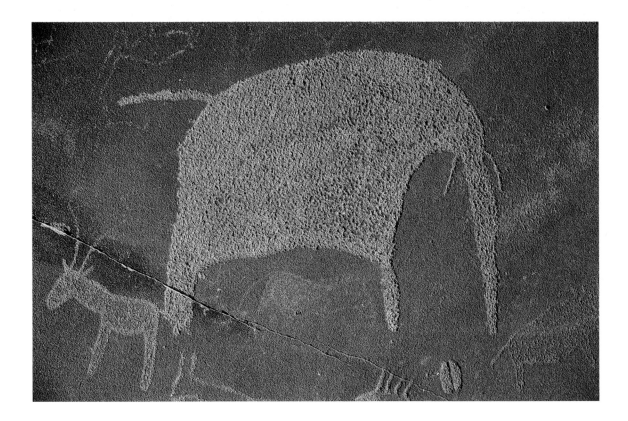

There are hundreds of carvings in the rock at Twyelfontein, set in a bizarre mineral landscape. These witnesses to early settlement were created over a period of thousands of years. It is impossible to date the carvings in the absence of the necessary parameters; no tools that can be connected with them have been found, nor does the surface structure of the rock provide information about their age. However, as the place was settled by many generations of people, these works of art can be anything from several thousand to a few hundred years old.

Damara and Herero people live in the villages of Damaraland. Often, the only adults around are old people caring for their grandchildren; many younger people have left Damaraland in search of jobs. They work in the mines of South Africa, or try their luck in the capital, Windhoek.

The costume of the Herero women dates from Victorian times, when missionaries' wives wore clothes of this kind. The skirts are made from a piece of cloth forty feet long.

Opuwo, on the outskirts of the Kaukau Veld, retains the atmosphere of a garrison town. It was the South African army base for operations against SWAPO guerrillas.

The Himba nomads regularly come from the Kaukau Veld to Opuwu to buy flour and sugar, or for medical treatment in the hospital. They pay with the money they earn from selling their goats to stock-dealers.

The independence struggle of SWAPO left
its traces on the lives of the Himba. The South
African army hired Himba as scouts to track down
SWAPO fighters.

Himba women rub their skin with a paste made of redwood power and butter to keep it smooth and gleaming. Their clothing is made from leather and skins.

The sacred fire that must never go out burns in Himba huts. Their lives revolve entirely around their cattle, which are both their most important possession and a guarantee of survival.

The headdress of the Himba women, the *erembe*, shows that they have reached marriageable age. Their hair is woven into long plaits with straps. After marriage, the hairstyle changes slightly, and two pointed locks stick out from the head.

THE SAHARA

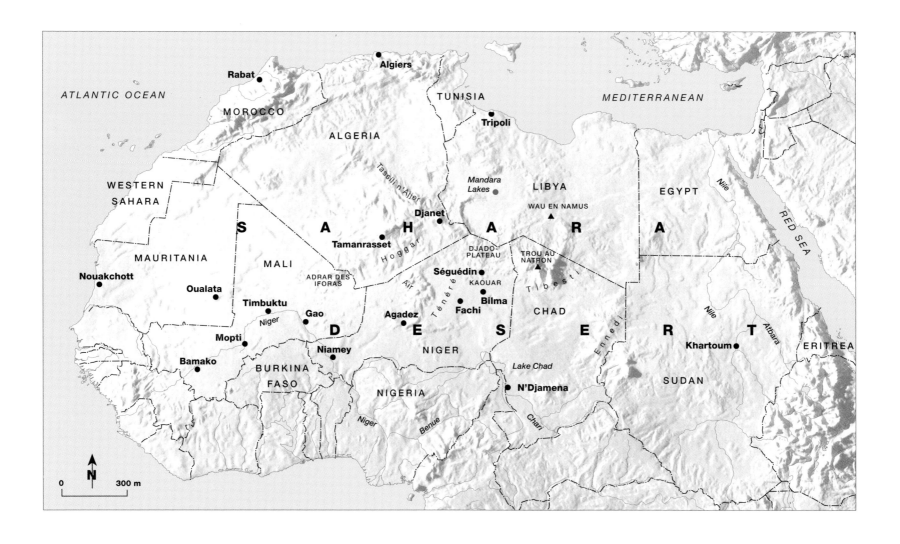

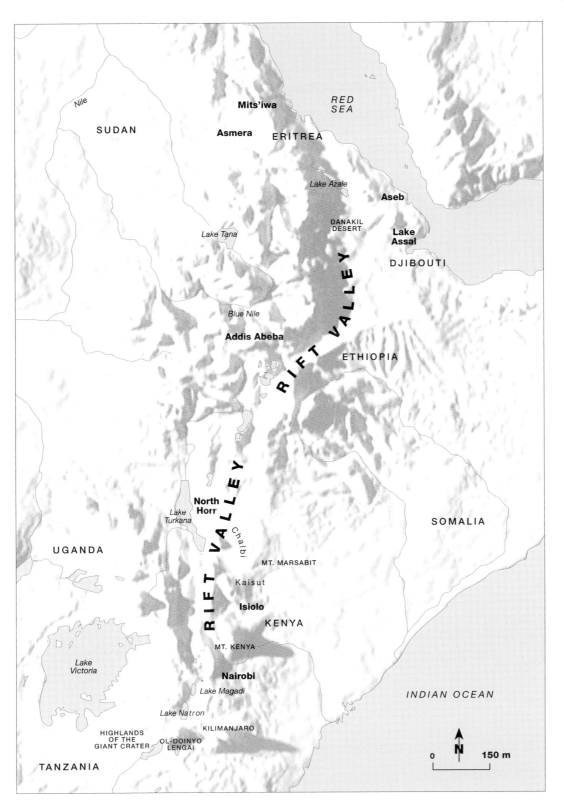

THE KALAHARI

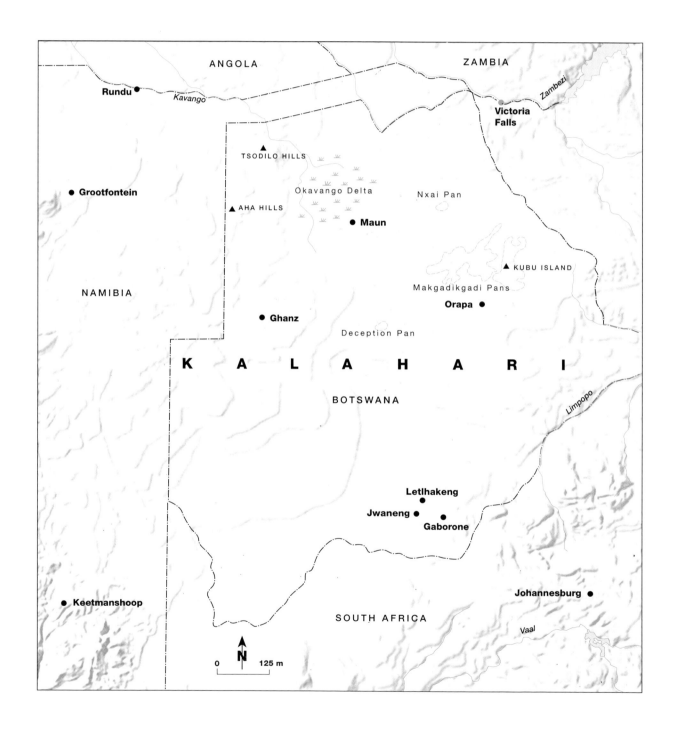

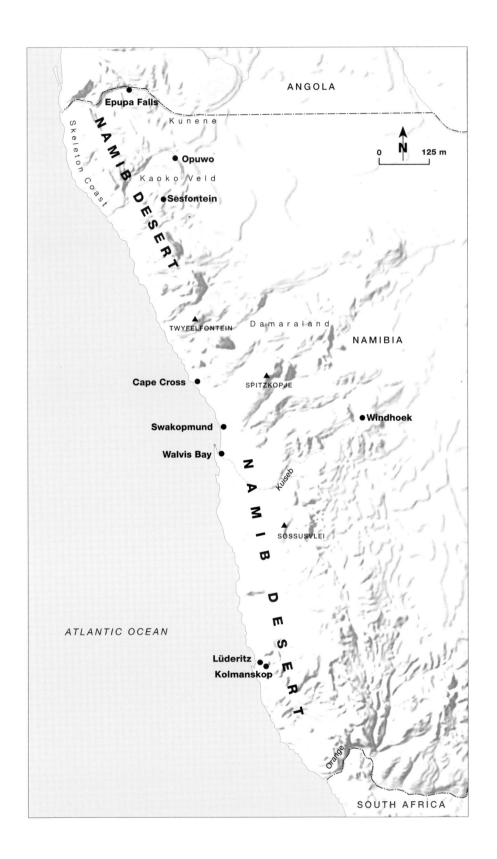

Ornaments

Allah is greatest of all / Allah is greatest of all / I testify that there is no God but Allah / I testify that Muhammad is the prophet of Allah / Come here to pray / Come here for salvation / Allah is greatest of all There is no God but Allah / Prayer is better than sleep

The muezzin calls the faithful to prayer five times a day with this summons. The five main duties enjoined on the Islamic faithful in the Koran are regular prayer, confession of the faith, giving alms to the needy, fasting during Ramadan, and going on pilgrimage to Mecca.

اللّٰهُ أَكْبَر   اللّٰهُ أَكْبَر
اللّٰهُ أَكْبَر   اللّٰهُ أَكْبَر
أَشْهَدُ أَنْ لَا إِلٰهَ إِلَّا اللّٰه   أَشْهَدُ أَنْ لَا إِلٰهَ إِلَّا اللّٰه
أَشْهَدُ أَنَّ مُحَمَّدًا رَسُولُ اللّٰه   أَشْهَدُ أَنَّ مُحَمَّدًا رَسُولُ اللّٰه
حَيَّ عَلَى الصَّلَاة   حَيَّ عَلَى الصَّلَاة
حَيَّ عَلَى الْفَلَاح   حَيَّ عَلَى الْفَلَاح
اللّٰهُ أَكْبَر   اللّٰهُ أَكْبَر
لَا إِلٰهَ إِلَّا اللّٰه

O ye faithful, a time of fasting is prescribed for you, as it was for your forebears, so that you may fear God.
You shall fast for a certain number of days, but he who is sick or on a journey may fast for the same number of days at another time. And he who is unable to fast in this way shall feed a poor man instead. It is even better to do good voluntarily. But it is good for you to observe the time of fasting, as you will surely understand.
In the month of Ramadan, when the Koran was revealed – as a guide to mankind and as the clear doctrine of the right way – let those who stay at home fast, but those who are sick or on a journey may fast for the same length of time at some other period, for it is Allah's wish to make it easy for you and not difficult. You must merely observe a certain number of fast days. Glorify Allah for leading you into the right way, and be thankful!

Ramadan is the Islamic month of fasting, when the faithful may not eat, drink or smoke between sunrise and sunset. Public life often ceases entirely during the day, and it is only after sunset that the streets of the oasis settlements are full. Since the Islamic year contains only 354 or 355 days, the beginning of the month of fasting changes annually by the common reckoning of time.

Arabic letter in the *tomar* style
Calligraphic Arabic decorative script
Arabic calligraphic sign for the invocation "O God"

Arabic script, written (like the other Arabic texts opposite) by a Sudanese calligrapher living in Munich. The translation reads: "Allah is greatest of all".

Battle rages at Amasara / The spear drinks Christian blood / The sword is drawn, and kills / And is withdrawn again. / Then I see blood before me, / it drips from my arm. Then it runs from my breast, from my leg. / I will not be bound with ropes / to be taken by the enemy. / Wounded, my mount / serves me as cover. / The young warriors of my people / fight bravely. / For each seeks a good place / in Paradise as his reward.

This is a battle song from the Hoggar mountains describing the battle against the French at Tit in 1902. It was composed by Sidi ag Sadáb, who was hit by 18 French bullets in the battle. The text is written in Tifinagh, the Tuareg script.

What is it, little one? / My good little one, / My brave little one, / My dear little one, / What is it, little one? / Be still, / I will stroke your fingers / I kiss the sweat from your brow. / I will stay near you. / You and I belong together.

Song sung by Tuareg mothers to their babies. The text is written in Tifinagh.

The motifs opposite reflect the shapes of New Stone Age rock art in the Tassili n'Ajjer in Algeria. The bull and the group of dancers come from Sefar, the archers from Jebbaren.

The motifs opposite show outlines of rock art from Namibia.

Fantastic human figure from the Ururu cave
Dancers from the Ururu cave
Figure from a group from Alettas Rust
Human group from Rooipoort
Human group from Alettas Rust
Hunter from Ameib
Hunter chasing a rhinoceros, from Nauzerus
Imprint of a hand from Witmanshaar

Postscript

Ever since I first visited the Sahara at the age of 17, the deserts of Africa have been a dominant influence in my life – even in the time between my travels in that continent. Something impinged on my imagination that was even more fascinating than the stereotypes of golden dunes, wild adventures and mysterious nomads: landscapes that could be found nowhere else, and from which one may read the history of the earth. I realized that here, where nature seems so mighty and inhospitable, it is in fact vulnerable and exposed without any means of defence to the destructive effects of human intervention. Above all, I met people I could trust and whose openness I learned to return. Despite their difficult living conditions, they radiated an extraordinary strength and zest for life. In the course of over 60 journeys, which have taken me almost all over the continent, the dignity of Africa has become my photographic subject. My pictures tell the tale of a continent where humanity and solidarity are not empty words – a continent that seems poor, yet is very rich. The concept and structure of this book try to do its subject justice. The pictures are accompanied by ornaments, examples of calligraphic scripts and background texts, eloquent of the poverty and the riches of the deserts of Africa.

Michael Martin
Munich, May 1998

Acknowledgements

Most of the photographs in this book were taken on twelve expeditions in which I visited fifteen African countires over the last three years. On my travels, I met people who made me feel genuinely welcome, and often gave me help when I was in difficulty. I offer grateful thanks to the following people in Africa and Germany.

Namibia: Peter from Swakopmund, who flew us over the Namib for three hours in his open aircraft. Mousse from Solitaire, who always welcomed us as friends. **Botswana:** Nixau, the leading actor in the film *The Gods Must Be Crazy*, who told me a great deal about that film. **Kenya:** David Allen of Nairobi, who flew us to Ol-Doinyo Lengai in his aircraft. Sode from Marsabit, who accompanied us through the deserts of northern Kenya on several occasions. The missionaries of North Horr, who always gave us a friendly welcome. **Djibouti:** the Somali mechanics Mahdi Sulton and his colleagues, who spent three days working to repair our cross-country vehicle. **Eritrea:** the people of Tio and Adaito in the Danakil desert, who encouraged us in spite of the mines and the condition of the roads. **Libya:** the unknown Libyan who gave us petrol in the dunes of the Erg Ubari when our motorbike ran out. Mohammed Tahar Ahmed Abaya from Al Katrun, who made it possible for us to travel from Libya to Chad even though the border was closed. Mohammed Ali from Al Katrun, who guided us safely through the minefields of the Tibesti to the Ténéré. **Niger:** the teachers at the school in Séguédine, who have their pupils' welfare so much at heart and who gave us hospitality. Mohammed ak Khabi, who waited for us for 13 days in Séguédine and then guided us safely through the Ténéré desert. Achmed Ewaden and Sheikh Mellakh of Agadez, owners of the Ewaden Voyages travel agency, whose good contacts ensured our safety in the Ténéré. Mohamed Founfoutou and Houya, our guides in the Ténéré. **Mali:** Alassane Maiga of Gao, my friend for the last 15 years. **Mauritania:** Sidi of Oualata, who brought us safely through the flooded dunes after violent falls of rain.

Germany:

Rainer and Sylvia Jarosch, proprietors of Suntours Expeditions, which organizes visits to the Sahara. They know the Sahara extremely well, and placed all their experience and contacts at our disposal.

Gerhard Göttler, the author of many books on the Sahara, for whose expert advice I was always grateful. I travelled with him in Libya.

Erika and Klaus Därr, who provided us with GPS navigational data.

Christoph Hofbauer, Klaus Hledik, Karl Johaentges, Holger Fritzsche, Wojo Kavcic, Alex Schwindt, Karl Serwotka, Daniela Schetar and Nicole Pramberger, with all of whom I have worked for many years.

The two qualified designers, Doris Jausly and Kay Maeritz, who designed this book of photographs. Kay Maeritz accompanied me several times in my travels in Namibia.

Herr Carl and Herr Heigl of BMW, Herr Hagenauer of Leica, Herr Rabe of Mamiya, Jochen Schanz of Touratech, Frau Trautmann of Air France, and the press departments of LTU and Air Namibia.

My publishers Monika Thaler and Gert Frederking; Christian Frederking, Ute Heek, Marianne Roth and Stefanie Segatz of the publishing firm of Frederking & Thaler; Daniela Weise, editor, Astrid Fischer-Leitl, cartographer, Karlheinz Rau, production, Dieter Kirchner and his NovaConcept team, lithography.

My parents Gerda and Gerhard Martin and my daughter Gina, who were my companions in Namibia. My travelling companions Beate Linsenmeyer and Wolfgang Kleiner.

And very special thanks to my partner Katja Kreder, who was with me on most of my journeys, and whose courage and capacity for endurance I greatly admire. Her professional advice as a qualified geologist was extremely helpful to me in writing the texts. This book is dedicated to her.

Facts

THE SAHARA

Location
The Sahara stretches for 3,700 miles along the Tropic of Cancer between the Atlantic Ocean and the Red Sea, and measures 1,200 miles from north to south.

Area
4.6 million square miles, larger than the entire area of Europe or of the United States.

Peoples
Tuareg, Tubu, Daza, Arab Bedouin, Moors, Fulbe Bororo.

States
Morocco, Algeria, Tunisia, Libya, Egypt, the Sudan, Chad, Niger, Mali, Mauritania.

THE RIFT VALLEY

Location

The deserts of the Rift Valley lie in the arid areas of the great East African fault trough, or rift, which runs from the Red Sea through Djibouti and Ethiopia to East Africa.

Area

Except for the large Danakil desert, the Rift Valley deserts are small in area, receiving little rainfall because they lie on the lee side of the prominent relief of the Rift Valley.

Peoples

Samburu, Rendille, Turkana, Pokot, Gabbra, Boran, Afar, Issa, Maasai.

States

Tanzania, Kenya, Djibouti, Ethiopia, Eritrea.

THE KALAHARI

Location

The Kalahari is situated in the middle of the South African subcontinent, and covers large parts of Botswana, eastern Namibia and northern South Africa.

Area

The surface area of the Kalahari is half a million square miles.

Peoples

San, Tswana.

States

Namibia, Botswana, South Africa.

THE NAMIB

Location

The Namib is a narrow coastal desert stretching along the Atlantic coast of Namibia.

Area

The Namib is 1,200 miles from north to south, and 30–90 miles from east to west. Its surface area measures 54,000 square miles.

Peoples

Himba, Herero, Damara, European immigrants.

States

Namibia.

First published in Germany by and
copyright © 1998 Frederking & Thaler, Munich,
a division of Verlagsgruppe Bertelsmann GmbH
Original title: "Die Wüsten Afrikas"

Photographs copyright © 2000 Michael Martin
English translation copyright © 2000 Anthea Bell

Published in 2000 and distributed in the U.S. by
Stewart, Tabori & Chang
A division of U.S. Media Holdings, Inc.
115 West 18th Street
New York, NY 10011

Distributed in Canada by
General Publishing Company Ltd.
30 Lesmill Road
Don Mills, Ontario, Canada M3B2T6

Library of Congress Catalog Card Number: 00-100212

ISBN 1-58479-028-8

Originated by NovaConcept, Berlin
Printed and bound in Italy by EBS, Verona

10 9 8 7 6 5 4 3 2 1

First Printing

LOOK
DIE
BILDAGENTUR
DER
FOTOGRAFEN
GMBH

LEICA